LAMBORGHINI
THE SPIRIT OF THE BULL

Paul W. Cockerham

SMITHMARK

This edition published in 1996 by
SMITHMARK Publishers, a division of U.S. Media Holdings, Inc.,
16 East 32nd Street, New York, NY 10016.

SMITHMARK books are available for bulk purchase for sales promotion and premium use.
For details write or call the manager of special sales,
SMITHMARK Publishers, 16 East 32nd Street, New York, NY 10016; (212) 532-6600.

This book was designed and produced by
Todtri Productions Limited
P.O. Box 572, New York, NY 10116-0572
FAX: (212) 279-1241

Printed and bound in Singapore

ISBN 0-7651-9626-3

Author: Paul W. Cockerham

Publisher: Robert M. Tod
Editorial Director: Elizabeth Loonan
Book Designer: Mark Weinberg
Production Coordinator: Heather Weigel
Senior Editor: Edward Douglas
Project Editor: Cynthia Sternau
Assistant Editor: Shawna Kimber
Picture Researcher: Laura Wyss
Desktop Associate: Michael Walther
Typesetting: Command-O, NYC

Photo Credits

Automobili Lamborghini
8-9

Nick Georgano/National Motor Museum
52 (top & bottom)

Winston Goodfellow
4-5, 14 (top), 15, 30 (top & bottom), 31 (top & bottom), 35, 49 (bottom), 78 (top & bottom), 79

Ron Kimball
28, 36, 48 (top), 58, 65 (top), 72-73, 76

John Lamm
*6, 10, 12 (top), 12 (bottom left & right), 13, 14 (bottom), 18, 19 (top & bottom), 29, 34 (top & bottom),
39 (top & bottom), 40-41, 42, 43, 44, 46, 47 (bottom), 48 (bottom), 50, 51, 53 (top & bottom),
54, 55, 60 (top & bottom), 61, 64, 65 (bottom), 74 (top & bottom), 75 (top left & right), 75 (bottom)*

Cindy Lewis
47 (top), 49-50, 67, 68 (top & bottom), 69

National Motor Museum
20, 23 (top), 24-25, 32, 37, 38, 45, 62 (top & bottom), 63 (top), 70, 71 (top & bottom), 77

Nicky Wright/National Motor Museum
16, 17, 21, 22, 23 (bottom), 26, 27 (top & bottom), 49 (top), 63 (bottom)

Contents

Introduction

The legendary sports cars of Lamborghini have been produced in Sant'Agata Bolognese, Italy since 1963. That the Lamborghini's history is set in Italy seems only appropriate, for Italian motorsports is full of names revered not only in that country, but around the world. Fiat, Alfa-Romeo, and Maserati all enjoyed grand prix successes even before the ascension of Ferrari, and did their part to fan national pride. These campaigns proved no less important than matters of politics, religion, food and wine, and music; the days marking the running of the Mille Miglia or the Italian Grand Prix were national holidays.

Up until the 1950s, the development of cars for competition and for more prosaic purposes had occurred along two separate, if not parallel, lines. Production automobiles were always subject to post-purchase modifications as their owners sought increased performance levels, but it was left to Enzo Ferrari to finally refine what were essentially racing machines with the addition of creature comforts, and so the gran turismo, or GT car, was born, bringing racetrack technology to ordinary drivers on public roads.

Built largely by hand and in limited numbers, GT cars could only be purchased by the wealthy, and were particularly popular among the new generation of industrialists who had begun to transform the aftermath of the Second World War into foundations for their personal success. As industrialists, they appreciated what the production of such an automobile represented; as self-made individuals, their egos were reinforced by the glamour and performance that such cars promised.

Such an individual was Ferruccio Lamborghini. Son of a farmer who made his fortune manufacturing tractors, Lamborghini had a

The distinctive lines of the Miura still look modern today. Many fans of the marque still speculate how the car, with its spectacular performance, might have performed on a race course.

particular appreciation for the durability of his products, and little patience when the fruits of his considerable income failed him. According to legend, it was a failed Ferrari clutch that launched Lamborghini into the car business in 1963.

The gran turismo car was Lamborghini's specialty and his passion. His ideal GT "must be beautiful to look at, as fast as a Formula One car, as well-built as a Swiss watch and as robust as my tractors," he once said. For more than thirty years, despite economic upheavals and labor unrest, Automobili Ferruccio Lamborghini S.p.A. has held remarkably true to that vision, producing cars that define the spirit of the GT like no other.

Ferruccio Lamborghini also had a passion for fighting bulls. A bull is found on the badge of every Lamborghini, and the uninitiated driver will soon discover that the bull is a fitting mascot, for driving the company's GTs has historically required considerable strength. Only recently were power-assisted controls added to the top-of-the-line Diablo, for it was feared (without reason, as it turned out) that such controls would dilute the spirit of the car. With power steering and speed-actuated, automatically variable shock resistance helping to keep its new four-wheel-drive on the ground, today's Diablo VT has become a civilized daily driver.

Technology has a tendency to become more accessible over time, and this has certainly been the case with high-performance automobiles. The fact that they must be driven with a tolerable margin for safety at speed led to the development of independent suspensions, fuel injection, and radial tires— basic components of today's safe, clean-running, and fuel-efficient economy car. Even cars as exotic as the Lamborghini play an important role in advancing the state of the automobile for all of its users.

The Lamborghini remains, both in style and temperament, a singularly aggressive beast. It has, for better or worse, developed a reputation in both the popular and motoring press as being the single most macho automobile one can buy. It is, more than any other marque, a "bad" car for "bad" boys, transcending everyday convention and fueling the dreams of enthusiasts throughout the world.

This 1976 LP400 Countach is one of the last built. Sporadic production could not keep pace with demand, and soon the design was upgraded into the Countach "S" model, with its relatively macho personality.

FOLLOWING PAGE: The four-wheel-drive Diablo VT is a miracle of mechanical engineering. Fully predictable and graceful in traffic, its power is now accessible to anyone who has the nerve to utilize it.

The very first Lamborghini was a prototype, the 350GTV. Built in 1963, this beautifully proportioned automobile had its debut at the Turin auto show.

CHAPTER ONE

The History of The Bull

Ferruccio Lamborghini was born on a farm near Ferrara, north of Bologna, Italy, on April 28, 1916, and grew up surrounded by mechanized farm implements, fueling his desire to learn about industrial technology, which he studied in college prior to joining the Italian air force. There, he learned various creative means of keeping aircraft operational, instruction which would later prove invaluable.

Toward the end of the Second World War, Lamborghini was captured by British forces and imprisoned on the island of Rhodes. Upon his release, he returned to Ferrara, where he started converting leftover military vehicles into agricultural machinery. The venture proved to be lucrative, and, by 1948, Lamborghini had purchased a workshop in Cento to produce his tractors.

Italy's desperate need for farm equipment soon allowed Lamborghini to indulge his own passion for automobile racing. He bought a 500cc Fiat Topolino, bored out the engine to 750cc, and entered the world-renowned Mille Miglia cross-country automobile race in 1948. The car retired with mechanical problems, but not before it had drawn the interest of several onlookers who asked Lamborghini for copies.

But as a budding industrialist, Lamborghini's interest, at least for the moment, remained with tractors. No longer converting military vehicles, his company was building new tractors from the ground up, and business had expanded to the point where, by 1959, Lamborghini Trattici was producing ten units a day, making it the third biggest such company in Italy, after Fiat and Ferguson. At this point, Lamborghini diversified into the home and industrial heating and air-conditioning business, forming Lamborghini Bruciatori. Thanks to an emphasis on after-sales service, this business also expanded.

With two established businesses providing a solid financial foundation, Ferruccio Lamborghini next tackled the production of helicopters, a life-long passion. His success also allowed him to sample several of the high-priced automobiles of the day available from Maserati and Ferrari.

Two events—one historical, the other perhaps set in legend—put Lamborghini on the course that would make him famous. First, the Italian government refused to grant him a helicopter license, which led to the abandonment of the helicopter company. The second event tells the perhaps apocryphal story of a Ferrari with a clutch problem that led to an attempted audience with Enzo Ferrari, from which Lamborghini was turned away.

Enraged, Lamborghini sued, and then decided to go into the sports car business for himself, believing that genuine concern for the customer after a car was purchased, and backing that concern with service maintenance, would prove a successful formula.

Construction had already begun in Sant'Agata Bolognese, a small town between Modena and Bologna, on what was to have been a helicopter factory. Now the new home for Automobili Ferruccio Lamborghini S.p.A., the factory was erected in eight months in 1963, and Lamborghini was ready to enter the car business.

As his workers had primary experience building tractors, Lamborghini subcontracted much of the work—such as producing the interior— that went into the 350GTV.

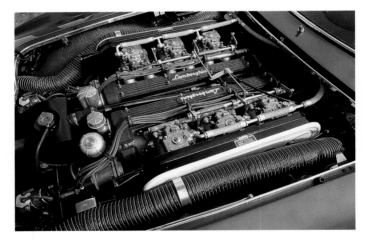

Giotto Bizzarini designed the 3.5-liter V-12 engine that powered the 350GTV. Its engine banks each had dual overhead camshafts, in a day when Ferrari engines only had one.

Lamborghini downgraded the output of Bizzarini's V-12 masterpiece from 360 horsepower to 280. Bizzarini, his hopes dashed that the mill would ultimately be used for Formula One racing, left the company.

A Magnet for Talent

Lamborghini was in a good position to build his team, for he was able to attract disaffected employees from Iso, Maserati, and Ferrari—particularly from Ferrari, whose temperament had instigated a mass defection of design and engineering talent at the time. One of those engineers was Giotto Bizzarini, the designer of the Ferrari 250 GTO, who went right to work and produced for Lamborghini a 3.5-liter V-12 engine that generated 360 horse-power, believing it would be used for a Formula One race car. Bizzarini later discovered that no grand prix racer was planned and would ultimately leave Lamborghini's employ (to be replaced by Giampaolo Dallara and Giampaolo Stanzani), but the engine was introduced to the press, mounted on a test stand in the newly completed engine-testing room, even before the factory had been completed.

The press raved. The magnificent and sophisticated engine boasted a pair of overhead cams for each cylinder bank, in a day when Ferrari engines only had one. It was destined to power the 350GTV, Lamborghini's first prototype auto-mobile, which was unveiled at the Turin auto show in 1963. The beautiful two-door coupe was designed by Franco Scaglione, and the chassis was engineered by Giampaolo Dallara, another ex-Ferrari employee. The prototype was large-ly assembled by the tractor factory in Cento. A badge, bearing a stylized inter-pretation of Lamborghini's astrological sign, the bull, appeared on its nose.

Only a single 350GTV was ever produced. Franco Scaglione penned the design, and the chassis was engineered by Giampaolo Dallara, an ex-employee of Ferrari.

The 350GT was Lamborghini's first production automobile. Its prototype was introduced at the Geneva auto salon of 1964.

Grace, strength, and beauty at speed—the essence of the GT driving experience, were well captured by Lamborghini's first production car.

For the production version, the 350GT, the Milan-based coachbuilding firm of Touring was retained, and by 1964 the first cars were being manufactured, with Ubaldo Sgarzi directing marketing and distribution. Sixty-seven cars were built the first year, a number that had increased to 150 units by 1965.

The next project Lamborghini tackled was a handsome 2+2 (four-seater) coupe with a 4.0-liter engine called the 400GT, which bowed in 1966. But plans were already underway for producing what would be Lamborghini's first signature sports car and the first of the modern generation of supercars, the Miura, named for a variety of fighting bull.

Carrozeria Touring of Bianchi Aderloni created the coachwork for the 350GT. The single headlights of this 1965 model mark a unit produced for the American market.

*The 400GT was a handsome, if
not somewhat cramped, four-seater
that Lamborghini first produced
in 1966. For this car, the company
bored out its basic V-12 engine
to 4.0 liters' displacement.*

*The introduction of the 400GT
marked the full maturation of the
Sant'Agata factory, as it was the
first car fully built and finished to
professional levels at the facility.*

Even though Ferrucio Lamborghini never had given permission for a race car to be entered in competition, that didn't prevent his engineers from creating a racing chassis, which provided the foundation for the Miura.

Largely influenced by the single-seater Formula One racing cars of the era, as well as Ford's world-beating sports-racing car, the GT40, the Miura legitimized Lamborghini's reputation as an automaker and revolutionized all concepts of what a street automobile could be. The 4.0-liter V-12 was mounted transversely behind the passenger compartment, and it powered the low, slippery coupe to a top speed of 160 m.p.h. Considerable technical input on handling dynamics was provided by Bob Wallace, a young racing driver from New Zealand who was the company's development tester.

As the Miura toured the international auto shows, orders from all over the world soon poured into Sant'Agata Bolognese, and mass production was ordered. As the exhibited car had only been a prototype, it took some time for the company's engineers to work the bugs out of the design, and only two production models were completed by the end of 1966. But the following year, 111 Miuras were shipped, and the car was a mainstay for the company until production ceased in 1971, with Wallace setting up the suspension of each car to meet the desires and abilities of the individual customer.

The seating position in the Miura is quite low: The two seats are situated beside two enormous external frame rails, the five-speed gearbox is in-between.

The transverse position of the 4.0-liter V-12 powering the Miura allowed for its gearbox to be situated in a parallel fashion, with power transferred by a crown wheel and pinion gear.

Rolls Royce, Italian Style

Not content with producing strictly sports cars, Lamborghini brought other designs to fruition as well. He had always wanted to produce a distinctly Italian answer to the Rolls Royce, a car that embodied comfort, speed, silence, and reliability. The prototype that manifested this vision was called the Marzal, and it proved to be a styling extravaganza, with huge gullwing doors that featured a large expanse of glass, surrounding an interior of four, chromium-silver leather seats. Built on a stretched Miura chassis, the Marzal shared its mid-engined layout, but it was powered with an inline 6-cylinder engine (basically, a single bank of the 4.0-liter V-12). The idea, when it reached production, became the four-seat Espada of 1968. An intact V-12 engine was used, but mounted in front. The Espada shared the same basic body shape with the Marzal, but did away with the distinctive gullwing doors. It was a roomy, comfortable car, a favorite with many executives who were Lamborghini customers, and a commercial success for the company.

The Miura itself was refined into the open-top Miura Roadster prototype, which was shown at the Brussels show of 1968. A fully realized variant on the basic Miura design, it was lower and wider than the base car and caused quite a stir at the show, but never went into production.

Another Lamborghini design produced during the company's early years was the Islero, launched in 1969. It was an elegant, front-engined car, built on the same mechanical base as the 400GT (which it replaced), with coachwork constructed by Carrozeria Marazzi. But by this time the company was

With its V-12 engine mounted in the front, the Espada was a roomy and comfortable four-seater that proved to be a major commercial success for Lamborghini.

Here is an extremely rare Miura convertible, most likely an aftermarket conversion based on a Miura P400S. The company had exhibited a roadster at the 1968 Brussels show; it caused a sensation but never went into production.

becoming known for progressive styling exercises, and it was felt that the Islero looked too conventional, so it was soon replaced by the Jarama, which remained in production until 1976.

It was during this period that Lamborghini fell upon hard times. The young and progressive company was subject to the political and union unrest that pervaded Italy in 1968, and Lamborghini, perceived as a producer of "capitalist toys" in a region of Italy where Communism had a strong history, was particularly vulnerable. Lamborghini's own strong personality did not lend itself to diplomatic negotiation, and he ran his company with a firm and unyielding hand.

The factory become the scene of daily labor unrest, protests, occupations, and the occasional act of sabotage. In this environment, build quality and finish issues, particularly with the interiors, became an ongoing concern; this must have frustrated Ferruccio immensely, as quality was a foundation of the factory's reputation. Now it was not uncommon for British customers, for example, to send their Lamborghinis to one of that nation's fine coachbuilders immediately upon delivery, to have the original interior gutted and replaced.

Compounding problems was the fact that sales of the Miura had started to slip. Despite horsepower upgrades in the Miura S model of 1970 (370 horsepower) and the SV model of 1971 (385 horsepower), a developing social consciousness made ownership of such an outlandish vehicle problematic, and samples languished at the factory and in the showrooms of the company's informal dealer network. But sales of the Espada and Jarama kept the company afloat, and advance orders were coming in for a new, smaller sports car, the Urraco. Powered by an all-new 2.5-liter V-8 engine with a gearbox mounted on the rear of the crankcase, the Urraco was designed to take on the Porsche 911 and Ferrari Dino in the marketplace; fine handling and a 140-m.p.h. top speed boded well for its success.

Lamborghini had envisioned the Urraco as a relatively inexpensive answer to Ferrari's Dino. It was unfortunately built during a period of considerable labor unrest at the factory, and its reputation for build quality suffered.

The Jarama 400GT was a replacement for the Islero, a design that Lamborghini felt was too conventional for its customers. This model dates from 1973.

An interior view of a 1973 Urraco P300. The Urraco was first presented at the Turin show of 1970; the car combined a transverse rear-engine layout (using a new V-8) with creature comforts for four.

FOLLOWING PAGE:
This 1970 Miura P400S is distinguished from early Miuras by its chromed windscreen, side windows, and headlight surrounds. The engine received new combustion chambers and intake manifolds; it could produce 370 horsepower at 7,500 r.p.m.

Disaster

The early 1970s were a crucial period in the history of Automobili Ferruccio Lamborghini S.p.A. Finally in a position to start making a return on Lamborghini's considerable investment, the up-and-coming company was beset by a disaster in the tractor division. An order for several thousand pieces of agricultural machinery, placed by a Latin America country, was wiped out overnight in 1971 by a political coup. In no position to recover any of the credit granted to execute the order, Lamborghini was ruined, and his beloved automobile company was put on the selling block, along with the heating and tractor companies.

These latter two companies, along with a 51-percent controlling interest in the car business, were soon sold to a Swiss clock manufacturer, Georges Henri Rosetti. Lamborghini then retired to a hunting reserve on the shores of Lake Trasimene, where he lived a relatively quiet life and developed a reputable rich red wine named Sangue di Miura ("Bull's Blood"). No longer involved in active management with the car firm, he soon sold his remaining interest to a property development associate of Rosetti's named Rene Leimer, who would

The Lamborghini Silhouette is an extremely rare, Targa version of the Urraco P300, powered by a twin-shaft, 3.0-liter engine.

attempt to develop a marketing alliance for the company in the United States with the DeTomaso automobile company.

But continuing union troubles, questionable management strategies, and the oil crisis would ultimately conspire to do the company in. The replacement for the Miura, known as the Countach (pronounced "coon-tosh"), had been developed and was first exhibited at the 1972 Geneva show; production would start two years later. A targa-topped version of the Urraco, known as the Silhouette, was developed and manufactured between 1976 and 1979. A deal

The Countach's ultra-futuristic appearance was abetted by the design's utilization of trapezoidal shapes. The clear fairings on each fender are for the turn signals, behind each is the port for the pop-up headlights.

with German carmaker BMW was pursued, where Lamborghini would have built BMW's M1 sports-GT car, but this ultimately fell through when BMW opted to have to cars constructed by a German firm in a more stable financial position. In an attempt to stabilize management at Sant'Agata Bolognese, grand prix racing team owners Walter Wolf and David Thieme, noted Countach enthusiasts, were approached in 1975, but persuading them to take over the beleaguered company proved futile.

In 1978 the company was sold to Hubert Hahne, a German BMW racing driver and Lamborghini dealer, and Raymond Noima, a financier, who in turn quickly sold it again to a Hungarian-American named Zoltan Reti. The latter persuaded the company's creditors, represented by receiver Giorgio Mirone and the commissioner Alessandro Artese, to declare bankruptcy, which they did with great reluctance on February 28, 1980.

At this time, Lamborghini was invited to regain possession of his old company at a fire-sale price, but stung by the fact that his volcanic personality had at one point led to his banishment from the factory, he flatly rejected the offer. The great man had burned the final bridge, and would never again be involved with the company that was so much a manifestation of his own personality. He died of a heart attack at the age of seventy-six in February, 1993.

Enthusiasts to the Rescue

What ultimately saved Automobili Ferruccio Lamborghini S.p.A. was the appreciation customers had for the angular expressiveness and out-of-this-world performance embodied in the Countach. During the twenty years the Countach was in production the company had rightly assumed the perpetual market appeal of what was almost always the fastest production car in the world—and that there would always be customers who were wealthy and self-

The Silhouette was a fine automobile, loved by its fans. When it was replaced with the Jalpa model, many customers ordered it with Silhouette-style rims and spoilers.

The low, slippery shape of the Miura—it was just 1,050 millimeters high—created a sensation. Bertone's Marcello Gandini took some styling cues from Ford's GT40, and refined the shape with hours of wind tunnel experimentation.

assured enough to fuel the car and drive it at speeds approaching 200 m.p.h., in disdain of political and social conventions.

Such was this appreciation that the two main Italian dealers, Emilianauto in Bologna and Achilli Motors of Milan, paid for Countachs in advance, knowing that they would sell to the handful of enthusiasts seeking the ultimate in exclusivity, and it was one of these enthusiasts, twenty-five-year-old Patrick Mimram, who stepped in and leased the factory just to keep the business alive. In 1980 the factory was put up for auction, and it was sold to the Mimram family for approximately 3.8 billion Italian lira, or $3 million (U.S.). Nuova Automobili Ferruccio Lamborghini S.p.A. was born.

Under the stewardship of the Mimrams, Emil Novaro was installed as president of the company, and Giulio Alfieri came on board as engineer. Production of the Countach pressed forward, and the Silhouette was relaunched as the Jalpa, with the addition of rounded lines, new rims, a spoiler, and a more powerful 3.5-liter V-8 engine. Simultaneously, development work was to begin on the strange and controversial "LM" off-road vehicles.

Jalpa and Countach production grew to the point where 280 workers were needed at the factory by 1985. The Countach reached its development peak in the Quattrovavole model, named for its four-valve-per-cylinder, 455-horsepower engine, and solidified its mystique in the supercar pantheon for all time. "Project 132," Alfieri's replacement for the Countach, was already on the drawing board, and it soon became clear that additional investment in the company would be needed, even beyond what the powerful Mimram family could provide.

At that time, Chrysler was in the process of rebuilding itself under the direction of the energetic Lee Iacocca, and was looking for means of enhancing its reputation in terms of engineering, performance, and the international market. Ownership of a specialized carmaker such as Lamborghini would help it realize those goals. Recognizing the Mimrams' willingness to sell, Chrysler announced on April 23, 1987 that it had purchased 100 percent of the shares of the company for $25 million. The company continued to operate more or less autonomously, and its brain trust remained intact, as would its identity.

The Chrysler years would number but six-and-a-half, but the company reached several mileposts along the way. A special edition of the Countach was issued in 1988 to commemorate the company's twenty-fifth anniversary, an aesthetic exercise that was a minor reworking of the Quattrovavole; the Countach would finally be retired in 1991 and replaced with the Diablo. The company would also formally embrace automobile racing for the first time, supplying engines to several Formula One grand prix teams.

Since then, Lamborghini has since gone through two more changes of ownership. A Bermuda-based holding company known as MegaTech, headed by Setiawan Djody, bought Lamborghini from Chrysler in December of 1993. Two years later, Hutomo "Tommy" Mandala Putra, son of Indonesia's President Suharto, bought a controlling interest in the company.

It is easy to understand the intrinsic attractiveness of Lamborghini to investors: a heritage for creating automotive designs that represents an absolute cutting edge in styling and performance—first fully realized in the production of the Miura, and ultimately, the Countach. Together, the two vehicles represent the birth and maturation of the supercar.

The 1965 350GT (150 units were produced that year) is juxtaposed with a modern-day Diablo.

The 3500GTZ was largely a styling exercise, based on the chassis of the 350GT, that paid no small debt to the successes Ferrari enjoyed with its world-beating 250GTO.

The Boroni wire wheels, bobbed tail, and "button"-style tail lights are but a few of the styling cues that Lamborghini's 3500GTZ "borrowed" from the Ferrari 250GTO. Only two were built.

Lamborghini updated the basic lines of the Miura in 1971 with a prototype called the Jota. In the nose, the fan intakes and headlights were recessed, improved ducting was found on the body, and a small spoiler graced the tail.

The Jota prototype drew much acclaim when it bowed in 1971, but despite this, only a single prototype was produced, which was later destroyed. The car shown here is a lovely replica, based on a Miura.

Gandini placed the radiators for the Countach at the rear of the car, making an ultra-low nose possible. Many who saw the car felt as though they were viewing an alien spacecraft.

CHAPTER TWO

The Bull as GT

By the early 1960s, international interest in what was known as the gran turismo automobile (or more commonly, the "GT") had escalated to a fever pitch. The genre had its genesis in Ferrari designs that originally campaigned in international sports car competitions and were later homologated for an elite motoring public. Enzo Ferrari is largely credited with creating this market, and nationalistic interest soon developed in knocking him from the top of the sports car racing heap. Aside from a few victories gained from the British marques Jaguar and Aston Martin, these efforts were unsuccessful. But by 1965, a Ford factory effort, commanded by the colorful and legendary Texan, Carroll Shelby, had reached maturity. The Ford GT40 won the 24 Hours of Le Mans that year, and the racing game had a new standard-bearer.

Ford's effort captured the imagination of auto enthusiasts everywhere, including the engineers at the new Automobili Ferruccio Lamborghini S.p.A. factory in Sant'Agata. It inspired them to create a chassis design that featured a mid-mounted (behind the driver's compartment, but forward of the rear axle), transverse V-12 engine. Dubbed the 400 TP (which stood for Trasversale Posteriore), the bare chassis was the sensation of the 1965 Turin auto show, but there were some skeptics. *Autocar* magazine, the prestigious British publication, proclaimed in its April 1, 1966 issue that the chassis would be a "dream car for a few enthusiasts."

Designed by Gianpaolo Dallara, who brought his aeronautical experience to bear on the project, the chassis was a jewel, weighing only 75 kilograms. It was basically a sheet-steel tub, with welded box sections fore and aft comprising a lightweight frame for mounting the engine and suspension components. The engine was a modification of the unit that powered the company's 350 series, with the cylinder bore and stroke increased to 82 x 62 millimeters, for a total engine displacement of 3,929 cubic centimeters.

What was most radical about the design was how the engine's crankcase formed a single unit with the gearbox and a limited-slip differential. The gearbox was arranged parallel to the engine crankshaft, with power transferred by a crown wheel and pinion gear. Other pinions drove the five-speed gearbox through a large, three-plate clutch, as well as the alternator. The engine produced 350 horsepower at 7,000 r.p.m., and Lamborghini stated this would push a GT car to a top speed of about 184 m.p.h. Girling disk brakes on all four wheels would reverse the process.

Such sophistication was reflected in the front of the car as well, where the radiator and two large electric fans were mounted horizontally above the wheel axis. Suspension geometry, both front and rear, was based on the 350.

For the coachwork, Lamborghini turned to the Bertone studio, which in turn gave the young Marcello Gandini design responsibilities. With only six months until the car's

All three sections of the Miura's bodywork could be dismantled to provide access to the supercar's mechanical components. Developing adequate cooling for the vehicle was a major developmental challenge.

scheduled unveiling at the Geneva show, Gandini found himself under considerable stress, but he recognized the car's mechanical heritage from the Ford GT40, and used the American coupe to provide stylistic reference points as well. The aluminum-bodied, two-seater coupe that resulted had an aggressive, slippery shape born of many hours of wind tunnel experimentation. The bodywork was divided into three sections—front bonnet, cabin, and rear bonnet—that could each be disassembled to provide access to the car's mechanics.

Cast magnesium wheels were used for production Miuras, replacing the wire Boroni units found on the prototype TP400 chassis.

Only ninety-one of the amazing Miura 400SVs were produced in 1971, as escalating social consciousness dovetailed with a saturated supercar market.

An Overnight Sensation

When the completed car bowed at the Geneva salon of 1966, the P400 Miura caused a sensation. Noted automobile writer Paul Frere would later observe in the April 15, 1967 issue of *Motor* that "In only three years, working from scratch, Lamborghini has come to the forefront of the makers of the world's finest Grand Touring cars, to be mentioned in the same breath as Ferrari and Aston Martin."

But transforming this wonderful prototype into a production car proved a tall order for the new company. With a large greenhouse and vast expanses of horizontal bodywork, the Miura required vast amounts of cooling to keep the V-12, to say nothing of occupants, happy, and it was left to Bob Wallace to spend many hours reconfiguring the cooling system, as well as come up with suspension tweaks that would actually keep the car on the road.

Consequently, early models of the Miura were not known to be particularly reliable, but the car's styling and performance were such that the company and its limited resources were compelled to concentrate on production of the GT for several years, so the car gained some refinement as time went on. The company's growing confidence in its abilities could be seen in the upgraded P400S Miura, which bowed in 1968. It boasted a chromed windshield frame and electrically operated windows, and its engine, thanks to new combustion chambers and wider intake manifolds, now developed 370 horsepower at 7,500 r.p.m., which propelled the car to the mythical 300 k.p.h. (198 m.p.h.) threshold.

The final evolution of the design came in 1971 in the P400SV, which had a rear track nearly 5 inches wider than that of earlier Miuras, driven by an engine boosted to 385 horsepower. It was produced through 1972.

The Miura also inspired a single convertible prototype that Lamborghini exhibited at the 1968 Brussels auto show. The Miura Roadster invariably fueled speculation that the company would mount a formal racing program. Many customers had pressed Ferruccio Lamborghini for special racing versions of the car, even offering

In case you're looking to pick up a used Countach and are wondering whether it will fit in your garage, the car is 13 feet, 6 inches long; 6 feet, 6 inches wide; and only 3 feet, 6 inches tall.

as much as three times the base car's price, but he had always refused, saying the company never had the resources and time to devote to such an effort.

In truth, it was never discovered precisely why Lamborghini shied away from racing. There had been some talk that he feared that his son, Tonino, would take up the sport at his peril; others speculated that Lamborghini, a shrewd businessman, observed the considerable expense Enzo Ferrari had incurred down the road in Modena with his racing efforts, and thought the better of it. In any event, the Miura Roadster never found its way to the track.

Changing social conditions both within and without the walls of Sant'Agata Bolognese ultimately brought about the demise of the Miura, but not before it had demonstrated that there was a market for state-of-the-art racing technology manifested in a streetable car. Part of the problem, too, was that the very state of the art was evolving rapidly on the world's road-racing circuits, and the Miura's design had dated rapidly. After five years, the distinctive shape was becoming perhaps a tad too familiar, and unresolved issues about the Miura's transitional stability at speed also dictated that a replacement for the car was in order.

The Countach

That replacement—the Countach—was in the planning stages by 1971. Many of the Miura's handling quirks could be traced to its engine's transverse arrangement, so for the new design, a longitudinal mid-engine layout was chosen. Emission controls were

The Miura reached its peak with the 400SV, which featured a widened rear track and greater performance, as the V-12 was upgraded to 385 horsepower. It remained in production until 1972.

now the automaker's lot, and Stanzani's engineering team confronted the tendency of such controls to sap horsepower by boring out the proven 4.0-liter V-12 engine to a displacement of 5.0 liters; the shop dynanometer indicated the mill was good for 440 horsepower. The LP500 prototype ("LP" standing for "Longitudinal Posteriore") also had a new chassis design, with a tubular space frame supporting a stressed-skin, torsion box layout. The gearbox was placed directly in front of the engine, and a return shaft passed through a sealed lubrication channel to the differential.

One advantage the layout posed was that the shifter would be placed right by the driver's hand without using linkage control rods, which tend to deaden shift response. The whole powertrain composed an absolutely massive unit, so the passenger compartment would by necessity be pushed forward, with the huge gearbox dominating space between the two front seats.

Gandini's creation of the Miura design had sealed his reputation; since then he had penned the Marzal and the Espada for Sant'Agata, as well as cars for Ferrari and Maserati. But the design he created for the LP500 was not merely unprecedented, it was outrageous. Broad, geometrically trapezoidal, sweeping, and futuristic, the car's most striking characteristic was the single flat plane that originated at the ultra-low nose (thanks to locating the radiators flat at the rear of the car) and carried through to the top of the windshield. Its huge butterfly-wing doors opened by hinging up and forward of the windshield pillar, boosted by hydraulics; its wheels had distinctive "telephone dial" rims designed by Campagnolo, the wheel arches that surrounded them were distinctively shaped in a manner that would become a Gandini signature. Pop-up headlights and fared turn-signal indicators were located on each forward fender, between which rested, under the hood, a space-saver spare tire.

Inside the car, the driving environment was dominated by the heavily padded gearbox, yet the sill sections outside the semi-recumbent seats were comparatively narrow, helping entry and egress. Digital instrumentation was initially proposed, but was nixed in favor of conventional analog displays.

The car's name was as outrageous as its looks. Its origin, according to Bob Wallace, came as he was driving the yellow LP500 prototype through the Alps on the way to its debut at the 1971 Geneva show. A resident of the Piedmont, spying the other-worldly vehicle, was heard to exclaim "Countach!," roughly comparable to "That's it!"

Stanzani and Wallace evaluated the design on two test tracks and on the hilly roads surrounding Bologna and Florence, and soon discovered (this being a Gandini design, after all) that the unique radiator longitudinal positioning caused cooling problems once again. Rotating the radiators 90 degrees and installing cooling ducts provided a fix, compromising Gandini's shape somewhat, if not making the car appear all the more avant-garde.

In the meantime, the production Countach was being planned. The chassis design was simplified, using a space-frame design and unstressed aluminum skins. The floorpan was made of fiberglass. The front suspension used double wishbones at each wheel, coil springs, fully adjustable Koni shock absorbers, and anti-roll bars. The rear suspension featured lower wishbones, single transverse upper links, and a pair of coil springs on each side to dampen impacts. Brakes on all four wheels for four-caliber discs came from Girling's racing catalog. Air intakes were added to the nose to cool the front brakes, and the roof received an even more flattened profile.

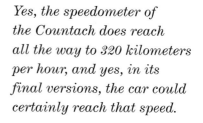

Yes, the speedometer of the Countach does reach all the way to 320 kilometers per hour, and yes, in its final versions, the car could certainly reach that speed.

The business office of the Countach is absolutely dominated by the central presence of its massive transmission tunnel. Because of its position, the transmission needs no control linkage between it and the five-speed shifter.

FOLLOWING PAGE: Here is a demonstration of the Countach's trademark butterfly-wing, hydraulically-actuated doors. Make sure your garage has considerable ceiling room before you pick one up.

Reliability Favored

The biggest change for the production model was the abandonment of the five-liter engine in favor of the proven reliability, and the readily available parts inventory, of the 4.0-liter V-12. Six twin-choke Weber 45 sidedraft carburetors, arranged in two sets of three, fed fuel and air to the mill, which now got its spark from a pair of Marelli distributors, rather than the single unit found in the LP500 prototype. The production car was consequently designated the LP400 Countach.

The first production prototype, in a bright red, appeared at the 1973 Geneva show. A slightly revised second production prototype, green in color, appeared at the Paris show that summer; it had bigger air intakes, a bigger nose housing driving lamps, and the single parallelogram-armed windshield wiper that was oddly destined to become one of the car's most recognizable features. The initial production model bowed at the 1974 Geneva show; it was ultimately sold to Walter Wolf, who would soon play a small role in the company's increasingly turbulent future.

Over the next three years, LP400s marched out of Sant'Agata at the rate of fifty units a year. Demand always exceeded supply, and the supercar game being what it was, it was soon time to upgrade the Countach. As both Stanzani and Wallace had since left the company, development of the new model was assigned to Dallara, who had returned to the factory after several years' absence.

Dallara intended to use Pirelli's new ultra-low-profile P7 tire and its considerable performance capabilities as the starting point for refining the new Countach, conceptually a new approach to design. The suspension was rearranged, and the Girling calipers were replaced with ATE units that grabbed huge, ventilated discs. The Campagnolo wheels were designated to be 8 inches wide in front and 12 inches wide at the rear, and the wheel arches received molded fiberglass fairings to accommodate the fat P7s. A front spoiler was

Six twin-choke Weber 45 sidedraft carburetors, three on each side, feed fuel to the LP400's mighty, and proven, 4.0-liter V-12. The Countach's prototype originally had a 5.0-liter engine.

The road beckons. Countach customers always appreciated the car's singular ability to command attention with its alien expressiveness and mind-boggling performance.

created by continuing the line created by the front wheel fairings across the chin of the car, and suddenly the Countach, now known as the LP400S, had an altogether macho look to it.

Components of the front suspension were relocated to decrease camber and roll angles, and the anti-roll bars were beefed up. In existing Countachs, high G-loads during maneuvering induced tire flexing, which in turn caused the rear axle to twitch; the fix saw the rear wishbones removed in favor of twin parallel lower links. Bearings, hubs, and the steering box were made stronger. Inside the car, control location saw improvements to help the uninitiated driver cope with the fact that, although its handling was sharp, and body roll minimal, the Countach was an utter beast to put through its paces, demanding both strength and sensitivity on the part of the driver.

By 1979, the Countach had become the LP400S2, which achieved a coup de grace in terms of stylistic outrageousness with the addition of an optional huge rear wing, mounted on the edge of the luggage trunk lid. With its inverted airfoil, the wing helped hold the rear end of the Countach on the ground at high speed, although it is an open question as to how many Countach customers actually tested this feature.

With the car getting heavier and emissions controls extracting their toll, the Countach's power output had deteriorated to the 340-horsepower level. At this point, bore and stroke were increased so that total displacement now measured 4,754 cubic centimeters, which boosted output to 375 horsepower. An electronic ignition system was installed, as were taller gear ratios, and the LP500S bowed at the 1982 Geneva show. Externally, nothing had changed, save for the car's rear identification badges.

For a while, the Countach 5000S Quattrovavole was the fastest production car in the world, and could be had for only $100,000.

By the time the Countach 5000S came along, a rear wing had sprouted, as had suspension refinements and lower body cladding.

The Countach set the standard for supercars during the late '70s and early '80s, with only Porsche's 959 and Ferrari's 512BB offering comparative performance.

The Horsepower Race

The Countach set the standard for supercars during the late 1970s and early 1980s, with only Porsche's turbocharged, four-wheel drive 959 model and Ferrari's 512 Berlinetta Boxer offering comparative performance. But Modena threw down the gauntlet in 1984 with the introduction of the Testarossa, whose 5.0-liter boxer engine boasted four valves per cylinder and output of 390 horsepower.

But if the Prancing Horse could produce a four-valve engine, so could the Bull. For the 1985 Geneva show, Sant'Agata produced a brand-new engine for the Countach. Pistons, cranks, and rods were all new, and the displacement was boosted to 5,167 cubic centimeters. The engine, named the Quattrovavole, also had four valves per cylinder (two each for intake and exhaust) and produced 455 horsepower at a silky-smooth 7,000 r.p.m. Breathing was improved with the use of downdraft Weber 44 carburetors, which allowed the car to produce an unearthly howl—music to the ears of any enthusiast—at full song. The car, now known as the Countach LP500S QV, again claimed the title of fastest production car in the world, a distinction that could be bought into for a mere $100,000 U.S.—at least for a while.

Ferrari soon reclaimed the fastest road-car distinction with the introduction of its F40 model in 1987, as the car's twin-turbocharged V-8 was good for 478 horsepower. Its body emulated Group C racing car designs of the period, but it offered very little in the way of creature comforts.

Sant'Agata was again quick to counter. By this time, "Project 132" was waiting in the wings to replace the nineteen-year-old Countach, but the company decided to tweak the design one last time to send it out with a flourish, and to celebrate the company's twenty-five stormy years of existence. The twenty-fifth anniversary edition Countach, which bowed in 1988, was fully kitted-out with sill extensions and color-coded bumpers. The interior received an upgraded air-conditioning system and electronically controlled seats (providing, at last, decent headroom for taller drivers), and the engine stroke was increased a final time to provide displacement of 5.2 liters.

Enthusiasts knew that only four hundred units of the final Countach were slated for production, but quickly came to terms with the fact that the $150,000 list price often commanded a hefty premium as well. There were some refinements for the money. The Campagnolo wheels were replaced with very light, two-piece O.Z. units, and further lightness was achieved with the use of magnesium for many castings, such as the sump, hub carriers, and clutch housing. With the passing of the Countach, Lamborghini had entered the contemporary era.

Pirelli's ultra-low-profile P7 tire provided a conceptual starting point for Countachs, starting with the "S" series. Here they are found on Campagnolo wheels: 8 inches wide in front, 12 inches wide at the rear.

The 4.7-liter Countach power-plant helped counter the effect that emissions controls had on the car's performance. A four-valve engine, the Quattrovavole, was introduced in 1985.

A frontal view of the Lamborghini
Jarama shows the car's unique,
half-lidded pop-up headlight covers.
This vehicle dates from 1976, the
last year for Jarama production.

A full complement of instrumentation allowed the driver to monitor
the health and performance of Lamborghini's V-12. The company was
one of the few specialty manufacturers
of the day to produce its own engine.

As the Espada remained in production for several years, many examples of the four-seater survive. They are a relative bargain on the collectible market for those seeking V-12 performance.

Several aftermarket coachbuilders recognized the superb engineering of the 400GT chassis and used it as a foundation for styling exercises, such as the Flying Star II that Touring produced in 1966.

The Bravo provided a passing resemblance to Lamborghini's Countach for the company's entry-level V-8 car. It could reach 60 m.p.h. in 7.6 seconds and had a top speed of 162 m.p.h.

The Bravo was a 1974 Bertone styling exercise based on the Urraco's chassis. Its monocoque two-door chassis featured extensive cooling vents carved into its hood and deck lids.

The rear wing of the Countach helps hold down the rear end of the car at high speed, it also adds to the car's overall appearance of sheer outrageousness.

By 1982, the Countach had been fitted with an electronic ignition system and taller gear ratios, and engine output had increased to the 375-horsepower level.

Even in white, the Countach's presence is simply intimidating. By now its front suspension bits had been relocated to decrease camber and roll angles, and the anti-roll bars had been beefed up.

Inside the Countach, control location was improved with the "S" series. The car's handling was sharp, and its body roll minimal, but for any driver it was a handful, demanding both strength and sensitivity.

This low angle nicely illustrates how the front spoiler of the car was achieved by drawing a straight line between the bottom of each front fender flair. This gave the Countach its particularly macho appearance.

Campagnolo had created the original design for the Countach's unique "telephone dial" wheels. These were replaced with lightweight, two-piece O.Z. units by the end of its production run.

FOLLOWING PAGE:
The badges and the rear deck are the marks of the Quattrovavole Countach. The decklid's two air scoops feed downdraft Weber 44 carburetors, which allow the engine to produce an unearthly howl at full throttle.

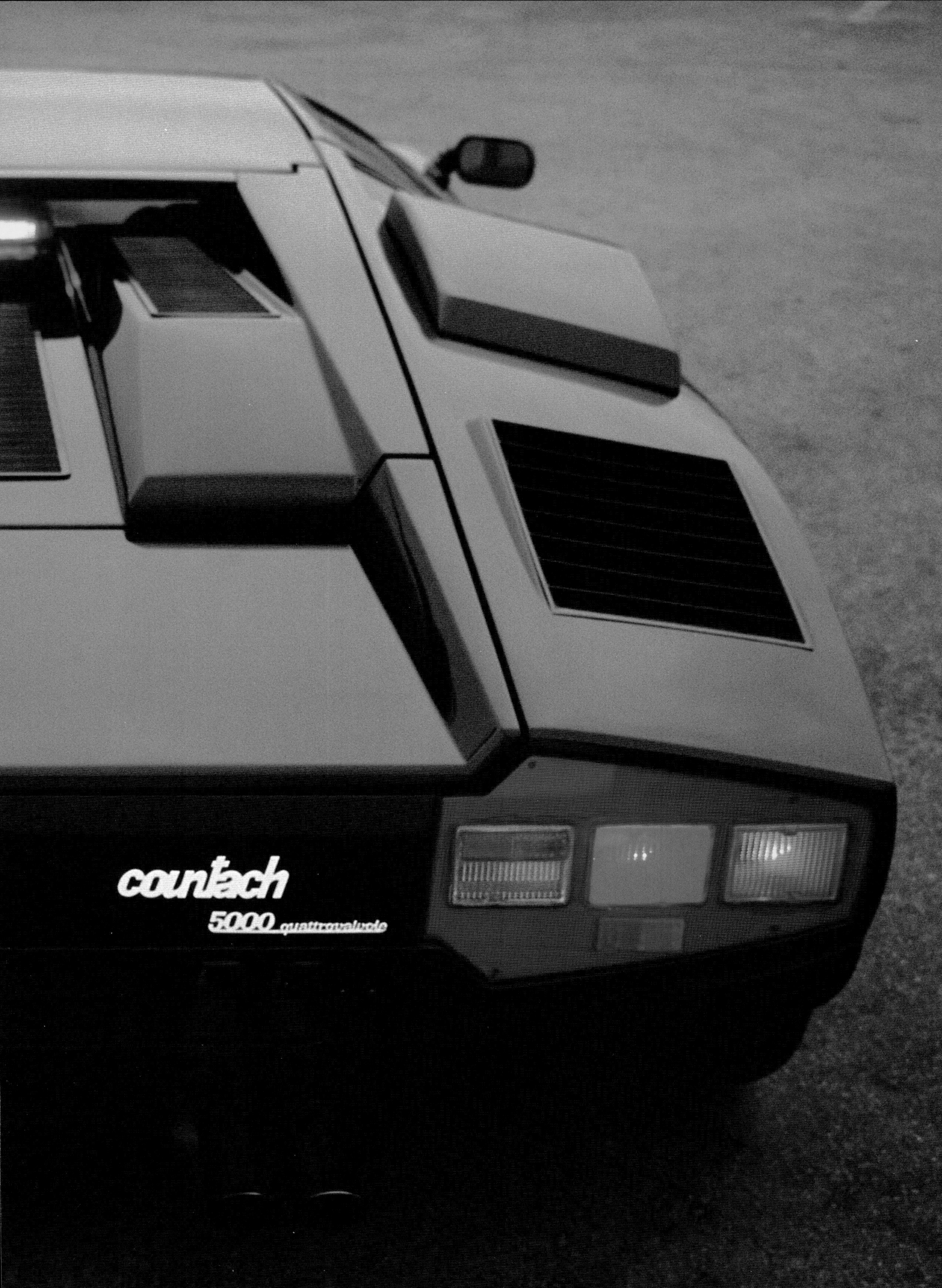
countach
5000 quattrovalvole

*The main underframe of the Diablo is
constructed on a jig, with chassis tubes
using a square, rather than round, section.
Its doors are stamped from a light alloy.*

CHAPTER THREE

The Bull Today

Recent times have found Lamborghini diversifying into activities both strange and logical, as well as maintaining its reputation as manufacturer of the most outrageous high-performance vehicles available.

One activity that Lamborghini's traditional customers might consider strange is the production of off-road vehicles. But always seeing itself as a marketing-driven company, Lamborghini responded in 1977 to a request from an Arabic consortium, the Mobility Technology International Company, to produce a fast off-road vehicle for the military market—the Saudi Arabian government was looking for a speedy border patrol vehicle. But the prototype that followed, the Cheetah, stirred more interest among the general public than it did among military generals. The blocky-yet-agile rear-engined vehicle was re-engineered for the off-roading public and re-designed as the LM001; production began in 1981. Two engines were offered: either the 4.7-liter V-12 found in the Countach, or a 3.6-liter V-8 sourced from parent company Chrysler.

The off-road Lamborghini was soon redesigned into a more practical vehicle. The new LMA prototype switched the engine placement to the front, and featured revisions to the suspension, chassis, and power steering. Production proceeds on the new vehicle, now known as the LM002.

The LM002 was unlike any other off-road vehicle. Its military heritage could be seen in its shape, which resembled that of an armored car without the gun turret. The interior was finished in hand-stitched leather and walnut paneling, and the mighty Countach powerplant (an upgrade to the 5.2-liter Quattrovavole engine) moved the 6,700-pound behemoth from zero to 60 m.p.h. in a mere 8.5 seconds, with a cruising speed of more than 100 m.p.h. and a top speed of 160 m.p.h.

As the vehicle was completely different from anything Lamborghini had attempted to manufacture previously, the company opted to have the chassis,

With the heart of a Countach, the LM002 could accelerate to 60 m.p.h. in a mere 8.5 seconds, and had a cruising speed in excess of 100 m.p.h.

body, and interior completed by an outside vendor—the Irizar body shop in Spain—and shipped to Sant'Agata Bolognese for the fitting of the drivetrain, electrical, and suspension components. The vehicle sold in the United States for $120,000, but was particularly successful in Arabic markets, where such noted car buffs as the King of Morocco and the Sultan of Oman are known to have purchased it.

The company also acts as an engine supplier, a role it has performed both for powerboat racers and several Formula One grand prix racing teams. Its history on the water has its origins in Ferruccio Lamborghini's fitting of two of his 12-cylinder engines in his personal Riva Aquarama motorlaunch, which he took to Lake Trasimene when he retired from the company. The company today supplies engines and gearboxes for both personal and racing watercraft, and achieved a milestone in November of 1994, when it was proclaimed world champion in Class One offshore competition.

As for automobile racing, Lamborghini developed in the early 1990s a 3.5-liter V12 racing engine, capable of putting out 700 horsepower, that was used at various points by the Lotus, Lola, and Minardi Formula One racing teams. The engine was developed for a cost of approximately $5 million—quite inexpensive, by contemporary standards—and in a realm where teams spend tens of millions of dollars each season in pursuit of victory, it achieved fair results.

But for the 1993 season, the ante was upped, and the company put its name on the line. In conjunction with parent company Chrysler, Lamborghini powered the French Team Larrousse, while contributing technical expertise and financial support for the 16-race Formula One season.

The interior of the LM002 off-road vehicle could seat four. It was an outgrowth of a border patrol vehicle design commissioned by a Middle Eastern government.

Immediate Results

The Larrousse team, whose two-car team had been competing as "back-markers" (cars that trail the field), benefited immediately. Lamborghini Engineering, headed by Daniele Audetto of Sant'Agata Bolognese and Michael Royce of Chrysler, created a traction-control system that improved the car's performance considerably, reducing wheelspin in both dry and wet conditions. Tweaks in the V12 engine's cylinder heads create a 7-percent gain in intake port airflow, and a 21-percent gain in exhaust port flow, resulting in increased horsepower during the second half of the season.

"By interfacing our engineers with this advanced technology, we stretch our mental vision," said Howard Padgham, a Chrysler executive. "Realistically, we don't expect to win in Formula One, but there's plenty to learn that has an application to regular production cars."

The team enjoyed its most successful race weekend in 1993 at the Grand Prix of San Marino. During a wet weekend, Team Larrousse discovered during the practice sessions that the traction control system worked so well that it found itself in uncharted territory in terms of finding a correct balance between chassis and aerodynamic settings, causing heavy understeer (where the nose of the car does not want to go into a turn) under power. In the race itself, driver Eric Comas was one of the three fastest cars on the track before being sidelined with oil pressure problems, while Phillipe Alliot hung on for fifth place, and the team's first points for the season.

Sant'Agata Bolognese had produced off-road vehicles over the years, the pinnacle of which was the LM002. This 6,700-lb. behemoth had a top speed of 160 m.p.h., thanks to its 5.2-liter Quattrovavole V-12 engine.

By rounding the lines
of the Silhouette and
modifying it with new
rims and spoiler,
Lamborghini engineers
created the Jalpa 350GTS.
It also featured a more
powerful 3.5-liter engine.

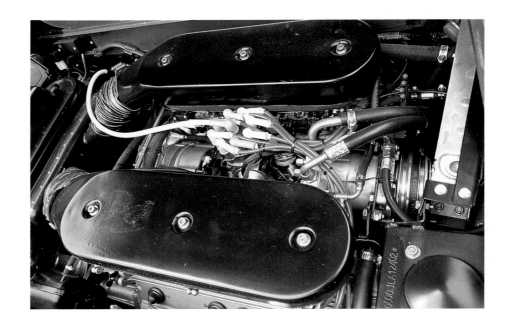

The 90-degree, 3.5-liter V-8 in
the Jalpa had a light-alloy block,
heads and sump with five main
bearings, and produced 255 horsepower at 7,000 r.p.m., and 261
ft.-lbs. of torque at 3,500 r.p.m.

The Jalpa 350GTS, positioned as an entry-level Lamborghini, achieved considerable commercial success for Sant'Agata Bolognese, as 410 units were ultimately sold.

In the cabin of the Jalpa, steering was rack-and-pinion; the clutch was a single dry-plate, hydraulic type; brakes were discs, fitted with Girling calipers.

"I used our traction control for the entire race," Alliot said afterwards. "While it did cause some handling problems, it was beneficial overall. Eric was among the three fastest cars on the track before he stopped. All things considered, we were pleased with the team's progress." The team was particularly proud of the fact that at that point in the season, it had motored past Ferrari in the team point standings.

But it is innovative passenger car design that remains the hallmark of the factory at Sant'Agata Bolognese, which has shown that it can keep in step with the world at large. Aware that the wealthy playboys who formed its core customer base might one day want to beget an heir, Lamborghini engineers, together with Chrysler, created a family sedan prototype that bowed at the 1988 Frankfurt Auto Show. Capable of a top speed of 150 m.p.h., the Portofino used the aluminum 225-horsepower 3.5-liter V8 from the Jalpa, and an all-alloy five-speed transmission. The open structure of its mono-

This ultra-futuristic coupe is the Lamborghini Portofino show car, a four-seat, four-door design exercise that appeared at the 1993 Pebble Beach concours.

The rear-engined Portofino shows off its most distinctive design characteristic— four butterfly-wing doors.

With its rear doors hinged at the back, the Portofino— developed with considerable input from Chrysler— dispenses with the "B" pillar conventionally located behind the front seats.

coque body and large, rotational doors allow for easy access to the four-seater, which also has a hood and rear deck that open like clamshells. Its four leather seats have individual adjustment controls.

The company also embraced modern design technology in producing Project 132, which came to fruition as the current Diablo. For a company that has always prided itself on hand-crafted automobiles (and even today, 95 percent of the assembly is still done manually), this was a historic step. "But it is impossible today to design and build anything without computers," said Luigi Marmiroli, Lamborghini's technical director, in an interview that appeared in the September 1992 issue of *Management Today*. "You need your hand and brain, too, but they are no longer enough." Using desktop design stations purchased in 1989 from Control Data, the Diablo's design is produced and refined in a relatively short time, helping the car conform to technical and emissions regulations in different countries. One particularly helpful function the computer performs is automatically triggering any subsequent alteration in the manufacturing process for each change in design.

But Marmiroli keeps his priorities straight. "A computer is nothing more than a powerful pencil—you can draw extremely clever pictures with it, but it can do nothing on its own—the ideas and innovation have to come from you," he said.

Gandini was once again charged with creating the shape for Lamborghini's supercar, and a full-size model was rendered by June of 1986. The exercise ultimately received refinement from Chrysler designers in Detroit, Michigan, but the result is a sinuous, somewhat rounded but still-recognizable update of Gandini's Countach design. The body panels are made of aluminum and composite materials, and the doors still swung up and forward in the butterfly-wing manner of the Countach. The seats, dash, and other interior panels are all covered in hand-stitched Italian leather, and the floor is carpeted.

A hefty, small-diametered steering wheel lies between the driver and a full panel of instrumentation. The five-speed gearshift protrudes from a chrome gate, and the engine is bored out to a massive 5.7 liters' displacement. The V-12 now produces 485 horsepower at 7,000 r.p.m., and the car is capable of a top speed of 203 m.p.h., or 326 k.p.h.

The new car's name received careful consideration. Company managers went through numerous volumes on bullfighting before unearthing the name of a ferociously legendary bull raised by the Duke of Veragua, "Diablo," which fought an epic battle in Madrid with the legendary "El Chicorro" in July of 1869. The car was unveiled on January 20, 1990 in Monte Carlo, and the workforce soon expanded to 459 to accommodate the ensuing rush of orders. Ninety-eight examples of the new car were produced by the end of its first year.

To pique the interest of those who dream, the company produced a roadster prototype in 1992, which was shown at the Geneva show. The following March, the "Diablo VT" was introduced at Geneva, and it was with this car the factory finally fulfilled its potential. For not only is the Diablo VT capable of mind-numbing performance in theory, it has become civilized enough to make that performance accessible.

"VT" stood for viscous traction, essentially an on-demand four-wheel-drive system. Incorporating components produced by Ferguson, the system utilizes a main output shaft that runs along the right side of the engine sump back toward the limited-slip rear differential, and then a second driveshaft runs from the transmission to a front limited-slip differential through a viscous coupling. Each differential has its own transfer and gear ratios, and because the car's huge Pirelli P-Zero tires are of different sizes and widths, the drivetrains are deliberately mismatched to keep shaft speeds equalized.

For the driver, what this complex system does is send power to the front tires whenever the rear tires start to spin on wet pavement, or when cornering at high speeds. The front wheels grip the pavement and rebalance the car's composure.

This feature, coupled with improved air-conditioning and power steering, make the car's power accessible to almost any driver who has the nerve to utilize it. It can accelerate to 60 m.p.h. in 4 seconds, and run through the quarter-mile in 12.3 seconds at 127 m.p.h., just when it has reached the top of third gear. But the car will still handle around-town traffic gracefully, a refinement not always expected of a supercar.

Of course, this performance is not totally accessible. The 3,575-pound coupe, 80 inches wide and 13 feet long, requires $239,000 from would-be buyers, prior to any luxury or gas-guzzler tax.

The company continues to offer conventional rear-wheel-drive-only Diablos for its traditional customers, those who prefer to hang out the rear end, wheels spinning, on a power turn. The Diablo SE30, a thirtieth-anniversary special edition, rolled out in the summer of 1994. Lightened, and with engine modifications that provided 525 horsepower, it offered acceleration that was simply blinding. Lamborghini customers also finally found that their long-held dream of an open-air car had come true with the introduction of the Diablo Roadster in 1996.

Known initially as Project 132, the Diablo was designed with the aid of computer work stations, which helped it conform with technical and emissions regulations for different markets.

The engine in the Diablo is a bored-out version of that found in the Countach. Now at 5.7 liters, the mill is good for 485 horsepower at 7,000 r.p.m.

The Diablo's interior radiates luxury, from the hand-stitched Italian leather covering the seats, dash, and interior panels, to the carpeted floor.

Gandini again created the shape for Lamborghini's Diablo. One of the car's most pleasing aspects is how the front fender integrates into the door panels and windscreen.

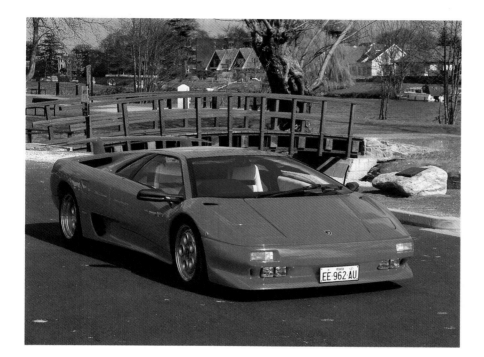

"Diablo" was originally the name of a ferociously legendary bull raised by the Duke of Veragua, which fought an epic battle with "El Chicorro" in July, 1869. The name fits the car's temperament.

The Diablo's lines received "refinement" from Chrysler personnel in Detroit, causing considerable consternation in the Italian press but still creating a sinuous update of Gandini's Countach design.

FOLLOWING PAGE: The Diablo SE30 commemorated Lamborghini's thirtieth anniversary when it was rolled out in 1994. A lightened car with a modified 525-horsepower engine, its acceleration was simply blinding.

The Diablo's body panels are made of aluminum and composite materials, and the doors still swing up and forward in the butterfly-wing manner of the Countach.

Still, the competition kept raising the threshold of top speed, and Ferrari's new F50, and McLaren's first production car, the F1, both beat the Diablo in that regard. But, of course, Sant'Agata would not stand still for this, and has developed a package that can be retrofitted to existing Diablos, or specified on new cars.

The upgrade creates what Lamborghini calls the Jota. It is officially offered for those customers who want to try GT racing, but it's not too hard to imagine that some Jotas will sooner or later turn up on the street. The heart of the upgrade is a multiple-mode engine control system which varies the geometry of the induction and exhaust valves. The punchline? Try 580 horsepower at 7,300 r.p.m., and 472 lb.-ft. of torque at 4,800 r.p.m. The plumbing of the new system necessitates a pair of bulging scoops on the rear engine deck, along with a deep front apron, modified body cooling vanes for the rear brakes, and a larger wing, so its distinction as the "baddest boy on the block" will be easily recognizable—no small consideration for customers, to be sure.

The Jota also features tighter settings on springs and dampers, variable anti-roll resistance that is controllable from the cockpit, switchable traction control, larger 18-inch wheels with bigger brakes, and composite engine and drivetrain parts to improve throttle response. All of this conspires to create a vehicle that has a top speed of 210 m.p.h.

With the Diablo Jota, Lamborghini has once again demonstrated a singular adherence to the vision of its founder to perfect the GT automobile, a vision that has survived union struggles, economic turmoil, and changes in management. As long as there are enthusiasts who can appreciate craftsmanship, performance, and advanced styling, the heart of the bull will still beat in Sant'Agata Bolognese.

A special badge proclaims the uniqueness of the Diablo SE30. Lamborghini offers a retrofit package for Diablos that creates the Jota variant, which upgrades engine output to 580 horsepower.

For those traditionalists who prefer to hang out the rear end, wheels spinning, as they power their way through a corner, the Diablo provides the ultimate trip.

Special cast alloy wheels were commissioned for the Diablo SE30. Purchasers should enjoy a special relationship with their bankers—Diablos now go for approximately a quarter of a million dollars.

The 5.7-liter V-12 in the Diablo totally fills the engine bay, and seems huge considering the proportions of the 13-foot-long supercar.

Five-point harnesses are found in the seats of the Diablo SE30—a necessary consideration, given the vehicle's blinding acceleration.

Even though its lines are an update of a car that still looked ahead of its time when its production run ended, the Diablo has a sensuous smoothness of line all its own.

*The Countach, which ceased production in
1989 with the twenty-fifth anniversary model,
provided considerable styling influence
for the Diablo, which succeeded it in 1990.*

Unlike many open-top variants, the Diablo Roadster boasts torsional rigidity as strong as that found in the GT coupe.

Shown here is the interior of the Diablo Roadster prototype. With improved air-conditioning and power steering, Diablos now have respectable street manners.

Lamborghini customers finally realized their long-held dream of an open-air car when the Diablo Roadster prototype was unveiled in 1995.

Index